Endorsements

"We absorb our mothers, / their virtues and shame, / their intentions and un-intentions," Deanna Shapiro says of her ambivalent relationship with an "unhappy" mother. These are the poems of a survivor: poignant and powerful, luminous and uplifting, always honest and impeccably crafted. In the many conversations, the poet-daughter has transformed memories of sorrow into moments of unillusioned joy—a stunning debut.

—NANCY MEANS WRIGHT, *poet and novelist*

Deanna Shapiro's *Conversations at the Nursing Home* is a collection of exceptional power that evokes the feelings of deep anguish in a daughter trying to anchor a robust will to love in the sea of her mother's resignation. It is a book for anyone who wants an authentic look into the human condition.

—GERARD BROOKER, *author of* Even Whispers Can Be Heard

Conversations at the Nursing Home offers readers the opportunity to glimpse reality as experienced by the person with dementia. It demands that we recognize the individual as a sum of their life's experiences and render care in a manner which makes this reality the best possible. It should be required reading for professional caregivers.

—NANCY SCHAEDEL, *Dementia Special Care Unit*
Admission/Program Coordinator

Conversations at the Nursing Home transfixed me. It explores the complex relationship between mother and daughter in language deceptively straightforward and disarmingly beautiful. Filled with so much understated wisdom, it is that rare work of art to be read and reread.

—RAY HUDSON, *author of* Moments Rightly Placed:
An Aleutian Memoir

In her book of poems, *Conversations at the Nursing Home,* Deanna Shapiro, chronicling her relationship with her mother and her mother's decisive dementia, asks, "How could I get what I needed? . . . How could she sew us/our necessary clothes?" These are poems that share what Shapiro—daughter and poet—saw, heard, and felt in those visits to the nursing home and to her mother. These poems let us enter into loss and what is redeemed by and through it.

—GARY MARGOLIS, *author of* Fire in the Orchard

This book gives a great personal perspective on the stages of this devastating disease from that of the patient, the family, and the professional caregiver. It should be read by everyone attempting to understand Alzheimer's disease and its far-reaching effects, from a real and unique vantage point.

—NEIL GRUBER, *Nursing Home Administrator*

Conversations
at the
Nursing Home

A Mother,
A Daughter,
and
Alzheimer's

Deanna Shapiro

PRA PUBLISHING   •   Martinez, Georgia

ISBN-10: 0-9727703-5-6 paperback
ISBN-13: 978-0-9727703-5-4 paperback

Library of Congress 2006929978

Cover design by Mitchell Stokes
Edited by Brenda Baratto

PRA Publishing
PO Box 211701
Martinez, GA 30917
www.prapublishing.com

Printed in the United States of America

Dedication

For my mother, Ruth Tornberg Klein,
who did her best and who loved nature,
healthy living, books, learning, and music;

and

for the superlative staff at
Porter Healthcare and Rehabilitation Center
in Middlebury, Vermont, with much gratitude.

Table of Contents

Acknowledgments ix
Foreword xi

Section One: Mother

How It Came About 2
Life 3
My Mother's Sewing Basket 4
The Little House 5
Circuit Breaker 6
Hymns of Praise 7
Remedial Awareness 8
Intentions 9
Blessings 11
Smile, Smile, Smile 12

Section Two: Mother's Family History

Steadfast Hands 14
Letter to Dora 16
The Wail 18
Necessities 21
Tough Times 23

Section Three: Conversations at the Nursing Home

Visits 1–70 26–95

Epilogue

Staff Memories 98
The Difference 100
Mother's Day 2006 102

Acknowledgments

The early poems about my mother and her family were written as a part of a series about my immigrant family. The conversations with my mother were written down after each visit with her at Helen Porter Healthcare and Rehabilitation Center, where she went after she broke her pelvis in a fall and could no longer stay at her assisted living residence.

A resounding thank you goes to David Weinstock for founding and leading the Otter Creek Poetry Workshop and for educating me in the ways of writing poetry and to my friends at the Workshop from whose comments I have benefited for eight years. Special thanks to Nancy Means Wright for encouraging me to publish my poems.

Thank you to Nancy Schaedel and Susan Corey from Helen Porter Healthcare and Rehabilitation Center for their generosity of heart and ongoing enthusiasm for this project.

Thank you to Lucinda Clark for her astute guidance in the ways of publishing.

Thank you to my husband, Charlie, who is my devoted advocate and who listens and comments on my writing, and to my daughters, Holly and Emily, who support me and my projects with their wisdom and love.

Thank you to my mother, Ruth, for trusting me with her thoughts and feelings. I hope I have not betrayed her and I hope she is happy to know that her experience may be of help to others similarly afflicted.

Deanna Shapiro
Shellhouse Mountain Farm
November 2006

Foreword

This book started out as a narrative of the visits I shared with my mother during the last fourteen months of her life when she was a resident at the Helen Porter Healthcare and Rehabilitation Center dementia unit in Middlebury, Vermont. As I prepared the manuscript, it occurred to me that perhaps earlier poems I had written about her and her family and my early relationship with her would be illuminating for the reader as well. Taken together, these poems shed light on the changes that took place within her personality as well as the changes that took place in our relationship.

Navigating the waters of Alzheimer's disease was sad and unpredictable; as the disease progressed, my mother became less lucid and less inclined to want to live. Yet the visits were interesting, surprising, and often funny and I felt good about whatever small ways I could make her more comfortable.

What I tried to keep in mind throughout the process was to respect my mother wherever she was in this debilitating journey of the mind; to enjoy the lucid, lively, good moments whenever they occurred; not to take verbal attacks personally; to accept her statements of reality; and to reassure her or change the subject when she was upset or depressed.

Through it all, I don't think I allowed myself to fully comprehend her distress. It was too painful. Many times when I walked out of her room and down the hall, it felt as though someone had just turned out all the lights. It broke my heart to leave her sitting in her wheelchair staring out her window even if she was looking at a beautiful cornfield and a nuthatch on her birdfeeder.

Looking back, I realize how much I savor the time I spent visiting my mother; how much I enjoyed that certain intimacy that our history together dictated. I realize what a privilege it was to share this passage with her.

Mother

Ruth's High School Graduation: 1929

How It Came About

As she slipped into the twilight,
transitioned to Depends,
gradually gave up wearing a bra,
make-up, scarves, and jewelry,
released herself
from her favorite talk shows,
movies, visits to the courtyard
to sit in the company of birds,
buds, branches and bark,
and then her beloved reading,
I, at last, had compassion for her
for I had transitioned, too—
I had built myself a house
with a firm foundation,
well-insulated, aesthetically pleasing,
a place from which I could care for her
and finally release our past.
One day she said,
The best thing I ever did
was to have a daughter!

Life

Something long ago
made my mother
step back from life.
She retracted her body,
shrunk into her skeleton,
and printed three words
on her forehead:
No, I can't!
That's what
I had against her—
for the anguish of it all.

But my body
rejected her message
like a transplanted organ
that won't adapt
to its new environment.

No, no, I shout.
I choose Life.
I choose Life!

My Mother's Sewing Basket

My mother's sewing basket,
a rectangle of beige woven slats
and orange borders,
held spools that discharged threads
hopelessly intertwined.
Pins and needles emerged
from a pin cushion lassoed
by strands of that jumbled mass.
Scissors and tape measure
lay imprisoned in this chaos.
How could I get what I needed?

Wild-eyed and tight-lipped,
caught in some internal web
by the threads of her life,
she stared blindly at what confronted her,
paced to and fro in the kitchen
or rushed down the street
leaving me to catch up.
How could she sew us
our necessary clothes?

The Little House

From inside her little house
I heard the raspy voice of a child-woman,
my mother, in my earliest days drawing me in,
into this house she had built,
where fear and loss played gin rummy;
a house big enough for two drawing me in,
to this place she called home.

Stay in bed, she'd warn me when I had a cold,
bringing me a bell to ring for food or drink.
Don't walk barefoot. Stay out of drafts.
No showers or shampoos. And put on your robe!

What do you want from my life? she'd yell
if I got in her way when she,
wild-eyed and terse, pulsed to and fro,
her distress mounting palpably,
over my brother needing stitches for a gash
above his eye from a blow in a stickball game.

I watched her, slumped in a living room chair,
staring off into space, absorbed in her thoughts,
some childhood misery repeating itself.

So I did the only thing I could do:
I soaked it all in, felt myself drowning.
I scanned her moods, adjusting
to her equilibrium. I held back from going
or went with trepidation. I shouted to no one:
How will I learn to fly?

All the while no one knew where we lived,
not even she or I.

Circuit Breaker

All my life my mother told me
she has needs which must go unmet.
Now at her senior residence
she has no one to re-cover
her Country French chair,
no words to respond
to Aunt Frieda's insult,
no way to find a new doctor,
start a book group,
have a bridge game,
no way to get whole-grain bread
or lightly cooked vegetables.

Her litany over, I, her daughter,
listening to this blasphemy,
riddled with irritation,
I, the congregation of one,
recite the traditional *uh-huh*.
No suggestions wanted.

After all, a need requires an action
and that is where my mother,
keeper of her light, trips the circuit,
all her life breaking the current
before it can complete its circle.

Hymns of Praise

My mother with her joyless ways,
regularly croons hymns of praise.
To others she does sing on high,
noting their skills, O my, O my.

Frances travels around the world.
Ellie summers in Chautauqua.
Helen plays a great piano.
Gussie is a balabusta.[1]

Fay's a great gal, never complains.
Pauline's friends take care of her.
Sue schedules family meetings.
Essie was such a stalwart soul.

O how, O how, Mom does beseech,
do these folks competently reach
all those sustained high notes of life,
when her range is limited by strife.

Inside her daughter's chest meanwhile,
Mom's own confined and hapless style
strikes major chords of helpless rage,
each time she sings her hymns of praise.

---

[1]Yiddish for head of a household; strong, capable, resourceful

Remedial Awareness
after Maxine Kumin's poem "The Envelope"

It is true, my daughters,
that you will always carry me
in the cells of your being,
willingly, ah, yes,
but also unwillingly, as my body
reverberates with my mother's burdensome
residence in me.

Like inhaling smoke from a room of chain smokers,
like ingesting the smell from pots
simmering on the stove, we absorb our mothers,
their virtues and shame, their intentions
and unintentions, what we like and what we hate—
in our muscles, our entrails, our nervous systems,
the vibrations of which trickle down
to future generations, our bodies imprinted
with the past before we have a chance,
comforted finally by remedial awareness.

Intentions

Just today I realized
my mother intended to love me.
She just never wanted to bring children
into such a miserable world.
She just resented my difficult birth.
She just needed time to nurse herself.

She made my baby food
and strained my orange juice,
stayed home from a wedding
to be rested for me in the morning,
rubbed witch hazel into my scalp.

Just today I realized
my mother intended to like me.
She just couldn't cope with the demands
that a child puts on a mother.
She just resented my place with my father.
She just was waiting to become her own person.

She dressed me in pretty outfits—
spring coats, hats and patent leather shoes,
and dresses with flared skirts
to hide my skinny torso.

Just today I realized
that my mother intended to do right by me.
She just was woefully undernourished herself.
She just swallowed too much loss.
She just had too many blocks
to her expression of joy and love.

She attended to my ills,
bought me crafts to take to the country,
gave me piano lessons and sent me to camp.

And so, just today I realized
I intended to love her, too.

Blessings

Yes, I've searched for, longed for,
blessings from my mother, Ruth—
for those certain qualities of tenderness and comfort,
vitality and delight that passed me right by.

And I finally found them in her African violets,
the ones she grows on her yellow iron stand,
that sit among teapots, a porcelain Chinese sage
and the rose quartz egg I gave her.

Yes, I finally found them in her healthy style of living,
yoga, walking, line dancing, swimming,
apple cider vinegar, kasha and whole wheat,
boiled water with lemon juice first thing every morning.

Yes, I finally found them in the books she loves to read:
Letters to a Scattered Brotherhood,
every night before bed, *The Red and the Black,*
from educational TV, the biographies of those
"who made something of themselves:"
Eleanor Roosevelt and Katherine Graham.
Like them, she wanted to be Ruth,
leader of her people.

But in these quiet ways,
she bestowed grace on me.
Yes, that I have finally determined.

Smile, Smile, Smile

My mother listened to *Rambling with Gambling* every morning,
our green Emerson radio
tuned to WOR. I swallowed John Gambling's program
along with my Wheatena
and Dugan's whole wheat muffins.
His Pollyannish stories about John Jr. and Missy,
his corny jokes,
his strident voice,
his sentimental music—Strauss waltzes,
his mawkish theme song,
Pack Up Your Troubles in Your Old Kit Bag
and Smile, Smile, Smile, felt maudlin to me.
I guess he energized her,
injected something positive into her day;
an uplifting friend.

Now I listen to *A Prairie Home Companion,*
my stereo tuned to NPR.
Garrison Keillor's humor,
his mellow voice,
his down-home music,
his stories from Lake Wobegon,
his easy philosophy,
elevating my spirit,
making me laugh,
offering communion.

Mother's Family History

Ruth, Al, Gerald and Deanna Klein, 1948

Steadfast Hands

My hands don't resemble those of my grandfather—
thick fingers, taut skin pulled over large knuckles,
hands that retrieved the money sewn into his pocket
by his mother on his immigration from Austria
to America, that said the final goodbye to his family,
hands that toiled from the turn of the century,
over thirty years, seven days a week,
in his New York City grocery stores:
lifting heavy milk containers into the icebox,
layering round vats of butter with a wire cutter,
positioning burlap sacks of coffee
near the coffee grinder, moving cartons
of canned goods onto shelves, packaging bags
of sugar from a barrel, candling and grading eggs,
pushing pushcarts, delivering orders to customers,
selecting vegetables at market before dawn,
and mopping down the tile floor each night.
Those are the hands that held his babies,
grieved when his wife died prematurely,
that pushed his children on swings
in an empty lot across the street,
and that held the newspaper where he checked the stocks,
grieving his 1929 losses.
In my childhood, I watched those hands scoop out
a grapefruit leaving nothing but peel. Tipping it toward us
he'd say, *This is the way to eat a grapefruit!* I watched those hands
swing at his side, broad shoulders, steady stride,
walking miles over city blocks and country roads. I watched
as they lifted his eighty-year-old body on chinning bars
in the country, he smiling proudly. I felt annoyed
by those hands pinching my cheeks,
their only gesture of love. *She doesn't like it!*

Why do you do it? my step-grandmother admonishing. He shoved
his first wife's gold watch pendant at me, my namesake's initials
carved on its face. *I don't want it,*
my eight-year-old sensibility said, pushing it back,
his hands roughly persisting.
My hands aren't thick and solid
like those of my grandfather, but the other day
I thought I noticed something of his in mine.

Letter to Dora

Dear Dora from Russia,
daughter of Jenny,
sister of Esther, wife of Morris,
mother of Saul and Ruth,
my namesake,
Devorah in Hebrew, Deanna in English,
you left us early,
peritonitis at twenty-eight,
and the grief, the grief
still resides in your great-grandchildren,
some lurking fear.

Devoted Dora,
pounding on Morris's chest on the street,
raincoat thrown over nightgown,
frightened by his late arrival
from a grocer's meeting;
coming home early with the children
from summer vacation
because Morris toiled alone in the store.

Beloved grandmother
standing corseted in billowing dress
beside Morris,
staring comfortably into the camera
behind pince-nez, you I have missed.
No one spoke of you after Morris remarried,
but he gave me your gold watch pendant,
shoved it at me at eight, sick in bed:
Deannichka, I want you to have this.
I did not understand, did not want it;
he laughed awkwardly.

Who were you, my grandmother?
Who might you have become?
What love could we have known together?
The darkness that descended when you left—
Who of us have ever fully recovered?

The Wail

Dr. Newman
The family rushed in
like waves breaking on shore
and embraced the two small children,
Saul and Ruth, like water surrounding
a sand castle built on the beach
by children on a sunny day,
when their mother Dora died
four days after entering
New York Hospital for Women—
acute pancreatitis, gall bladder surgery,
peritonitis dooming her finally.
Be a good boy, she murmured to Saul,
the elder at four, patting him on the head
when they brought the children
to say good-bye.

Dora
I was cut down just as I was flowering,
with two beautiful children and a handsome,
hardworking husband. We were making our way
in the new world together. How will
my adored family survive? They need someone
as devoted as I was. I worried over their every move.
Morris knows nothing about children. I was so ill.
The pain was so great, but the psychic pain
was greater.

Jenny
I survived Russian pogroms,
my trip to America, two husbands,
but, oh, my daughter's death!
My life went with her.

Why didn't He take me?
For the rest of my years I cried
over Dora's daughter,
that poor orphan. *Poor Ruthie,*
Dora's daughter, was my mantra
as though Ruthie was the mausoleum
that encrypted Dora.

Esther
My adored older sister was gone—
so stable, so responsible;
I counted on her. They wanted me
to take her place, to marry Morris.
How could I? But I had to care
for her children. So I married his brother Harry,
not as strong as Morris, but not as serious—
lighthearted and impish. And we took care
of Dora's children like our own.

Mendel
I was her older brother, the man of the family.
What could I have done?
Wife, mother, homemaker—none
could replace her. I heard of a widow
with a daughter in Philadelphia.
She had been married to a distant relative.
Maybe Fanny could marry Morris.
Maybe they could make a family
out of this rubble.

Fanny
I lost my first love. He read me poetry.
I will never love again. But I was a widow
with a daughter. Never mind sentiment.
I needed to provide for Teenie.
Where was I to go? Morris was a decent man.

However unsuited we were for each other,
we had to make this work.

Morris

The love of my life was gone.
Do you know how much she loved me?
I'll never find another like her.
I plunged myself into my grocery store—
those long, cool hours distracted me.
I churned the hot ashes of my grief
in silence. I had to find a caretaker
for my children. Fanny was a stoic woman.
But don't mistake my silence for contentment.

Saul

I lost my sweet mama,
that angel that watched over us.
My grief turned to anger.
I overslept, was late to school,
roamed the streets, didn't come home,
wasn't there to help in the store.
I ate food that upset my stomach.
I drove them all crazy.

Ruth

Oy gevalt! A cold wind
slammed our front door shut
and the lights went out
when my poor mama died.
They all tried to help me,
fed my sickly body, invited me over.
But I never recovered. I was always
poor Ruthie, Dora's daughter.
I was, though I hated it!

Necessities

I

It isn't necessary, her stepmother said,
to have a doll, ice cream replaced
that fell off its cone, money for candy,
more than a box of Nabisco Sugar Wafers
for a friend on her birthday,
to dress like your friends and go downtown.
So after awhile my mother stopped asking,
walked to school to save a nickel carfare
and bought a candy bar.
Her friends shouted, *Hurray!*
Her first boss asked, *Does she have any clothes?*

II

What was necessary after all?
For her father to work night and day
in his grocery?
For her stepmother to give the cream
on top of the milk to her children?
For them to neglect her sore throat
leading to pneumonia and mastoid surgery?
For her to be introduced
as *poor Ruthie, Dora's daughter?*

III

Yes, but what was necessary
for these young parents in a new land,
hardworking, raising four children
in an arranged marriage, first loves lost,
she complaining about his silence,
he shrugging, turning red
in embarrassed laughter.

IV

Who of them knew what was necessary
for a sickly, depressed girl, mother lost at age two,
for an immigrant family with a pocket full of losses?

Tough Times

My mother secured an office job in stationery supply
in 1929, though times were tough, after graduating
from James Monroe High School
with a bookkeeping medal.
Her soft beauty stares out at the onlooker
from her graduation portrait, she,
dressed in white chiffon,
three bands of white ribbon
spanning her dark brown hair,
standing beside a pedestal with a vase
of white flowers,
her lackluster eyes, unsmiling face
still reflecting the loss
of her mother at age two,
her sickly, deprived childhood.
She gave her salary to her parents
(later used for her wedding and furniture)
and got a weekly allowance.
Times were tough, but for her, nothing was different.

My father got a job with Tousch-Niven,
an accounting firm, in 1929,
though times were tough,
graduating the year before from NYU night school
the first in his family; bright eyes and half-smile
in his graduation portrait greet the onlooker
with optimism, the satisfaction of success.
He, working at that firm for eight years,
finally met my mother at Bachman-Emerich,
where he went to do an audit,
wrote her a letter from out-of-town
two weeks later. *I bet he asks you to marry him,*
her stepmother said. *Don't be silly,* she replied.

Indeed, he'd proposed. *I solicit an answer,*
was what he wrote.

Still living at home, all siblings married,
he succumbed to her beauty, her quiet demeanor,
that would fit with his, allow him to lead. She,
all her friends married, decided, like him,
it was time for a stable companion,
strangers though they were.

And that is how my father became accountable
for an unhappy woman for fifty-four years.

Conversations
at the Nursing Home

Ruth and Deanna: 2004

June 2004

VISIT 1

My ninety-two-year-old mother
is still in her nightgown when I visit her
at the nursing home. It is three o'clock.
"I'm rebelling," she says, seeing me enter.
She has refused to get up, refused her meals.
"They won't let me go to New York."
"What's in New York?" I ask.
"My partner."
"Who is your partner?"
"You know," she glares.
"I don't," I reply.
"Who is your partner?"
"At-the-cem-e-ter-y!" she enunciates
slowly, leering at me.
"You have to die first," I remind her.
"I know," she says half-heartedly.
"So when will that happen?"
"I don't know," she says wearily.

VISIT 2

"Look at her!" my mother says condescendingly
as we sit in the dementia unit day room.
"She dresses in that costume every day!
No one knows where she goes or what she does."
The woman in question wears a long jeans skirt,
several long-sleeve tops, and the long plaid bib
worn at meal time. Eyes dull, rimmed in red,
hair lifelessly framing her face, she walks
the halls, perches briefly on a chair,
walks again, repeating her pattern all day.
"That's part of her illness," I say quietly.
"Illness!" my mother is shocked.
"You mean she is a guest here?"

VISIT 3

"I want a different partner," my mother says.
"You mean roommate?" I ask.
"Yes. I think this one left."
"No, she is still here."
"She is?" she says disgustedly.
"Yes," I assure her, having seen her diminutive,
white-haired roommate in the hall.
"I can't stand her blue mattress! They put it
on the floor near her bed in case she rolls out
at night. Then they stand it up
in middle of our room during the day.
I wish they'd get it out of here!"
"Have you ever spoken to her?"
"No. She doesn't appeal to me.
I know. It's my fault."

VISIT 4

"I want to go inside soon," my mother says.
We are sitting in the courtyard, watching
the birds and chipmunks, listening
to the water fountain gurgle, talking.
"It's early for your dinner," I reply.
"I know. But I want to get a place
at the small table. I don't like eating
at the large table."
"Why not?"
"The people that sit there need to be fed.
It turns my stomach."

July 2004

VISIT 5

"Look. You see her, with the blue belt?
All the people here with blue belts
are Jewish," my mother says.
She is referring to the residents
in wheelchairs who are strapped in
with blue belts so they won't fall out.
She has lived a lifetime among Jews
and now she is the only Jew here.

VISIT 6

"My neuropathy is bothering me.
The doctor wants to give me
more Tylenol."
"Well, will you take it?"
"I'm thinking it over."
"You want to die anyway.
So why not be comfortable
in the meantime?"
No answer.

VISIT 7

"They give me so many pills here.
They're always giving me pills.
I used to take a Tylenol myself
if the neuropathy bothered me.
Now they give me two in the morning
and two at night."
"Are you taking them?"
"Yes. I don't want to live forever."

August 2004

VISIT 8

"It's not too bad here."
"What do you mean?"
"Well, it's amusing."
"Amusing?"
"Watching the inmates and the girls.
If they're grumpy, they kiss them
to get them to do what they want.
If they don't want to eat, a girl
feeds them. They won't open
their mouths! If they didn't open
their mouths for me, they'd starve!
It's the worst job in the world.
It's the last one I'd ever want.
Wouldn't want it, no way.
Washing people, feeding them,
taking them to the bathroom.
It's hard. But they love it!"

VISIT 9

"All they do here is sleep.
They sleep when they eat.
They sleep playing games.
They sleep at exercise class.
One other woman and I do
the exercises. They're always
sleeping. They sleep.
I read."

VISIT 10

"I almost left today."
"How come?"
"My partner had company
and I wanted to read and sleep.
They wouldn't stop talking."
"Who was her company?"
"Her mother, her parents.
They were talking so loud.
So I packed up—the children,
everything. But then
they finally left. Everyone
was glad when I unpacked."

VISIT 11

"When I get my food I know
what I'm doing. I eat
and get finished. The others
take forever. They have to be fed.
The girls put ice cream
on the spoon with the vegetables
so they'll eat. I can't get over it.
They won't eat! I just get to work
and finish. I hope they don't think
it's because I'm Jewish."

VISIT 12

"The new girls say, 'That girl
is Jewish.' Not the older girls.
Just the new ones."
"Why?" I ask.
"I don't know. I've been reading
in my Hadassah magazine
about the Jews in Europe.
Who would have thought
this would happen again?"
"Especially in France."
"Who would have imagined?"
shaking her head.

September 2004

VISIT 13

"They show partiality here."
"What do you mean?"
"I mean I get different things
to eat than the others."
"But you asked for fruit
and vegetables and no meat."
"I know, but now I want a little meat
and they still don't give it to me."
"Why would they be partial?"
"Because I'm Jewish.
There are others here who are Jewish,
but they don't say anything.
I tell them I'm Jewish."

VISIT 14

"Yes," my mother says, when I ask
if she'd like to go out in the courtyard—
then maneuvers her wheelchair
next to Tim. "Would you like to come
out to the courtyard with us?
Why don't you come out? You'll like it."
He looks at her blankly, attempts
to say something, and fails.
"Why do you fall asleep when you eat?"
she continues. "You shouldn't do that."
"Mom, I can't manage two wheelchairs.
Someone else will have to take Tim out."
"Get someone to take you out," she says.
"One of the girls will do it. Just ask them.
They'll do it."
He stares at her with furrowed brow.

VISIT 15

"I wanted to ask you about these books I'm reading.
Do you think it was right for Nelson Mandela
to leave his children to be leader of his movement?"
"It's the kind of decision people have to make
for themselves."
"I know, but he hardly saw his children all those years."
"That was a big price to pay."
"But I wanted to know what you thought about that."
"I don't know what I would have done.
It's a very hard decision."

Nurse Report: "Your mother slid out of her wheelchair last night but she refused help. She wasn't hurt, but she wouldn't let us touch her. Finally, we calmed her down and helped her up."

VISIT 16

"I just started this other book
and it makes me feel peculiar.
He's talking about Christian theories
and behavior. And he quotes
Christian theologians who agree with him."
"Well, if you read the book it might help you
understand more about Christian beliefs."
"And he says these are the only true values—
the ones from the New Testament.
It makes me feel peculiar."
"Some Christian beliefs are similar
to Jewish beliefs. But you don't feel
acknowledged as a Jew in that book."
"That's right and I don't have enough background
to sort it out."
"Well, if you don't feel comfortable with it,
you don't have to read it."
"That's just it. I don't feel comfortable either way.
If I read it, I don't feel comfortable,
and if I don't read it, maybe it's because
I'm just shying away from it."
"Why don't you talk to the chaplain about it
since she brought you the book?"
"I don't know why she gave me this book."

October 2004

VISIT 17

"The people here are so cranky and dull.
They're not motivated. They just sleep.
At night they're cranky when they wait
to get taken to their rooms. So they give them
a piece of cheese or ice cream.
We need kazoos. That'll wake everyone up!"

VISIT 18

"Some of the girls hold dolls.
All day long they hold these dolls.
I never saw such real dolls.
One of them holds a dog.
It's pathetic!"

VISIT 19

"How is the yoga exercise class?" I ask.
"It's not like the yoga I was used to."
"Well, they've adapted it for people
in wheelchairs."
"I know. But the handicapped people
limit it. A new woman joined the group.
She has a doll. All she does is talk to the doll
and feed the doll. I told the teacher
it was distracting. 'Why is it distracting?'
she asked me. So I let it go.
I think they try to gather as many people
in there as they can."
"Well, they are trying to benefit the residents,
trying to draw them out. But I know
it impacts you."
"Yes. Another woman wedged her wheelchair
in near me. I said to her, 'Are you expecting
to do the exercises?' She just glared at me.
I suppose it helps you to see
what other people are up against."

Director Report: "We got a grant to do a memories project
with some residents. It involves painting. I wonder if we
could have permission to include your mother. We think
she'd do very well with it."
"That would be wonderful! But I don't know if you can get
her to participate. It's not her thing."
"We're discussing our approach with the residents now. So
you can leave that up to us."

VISIT 20

"There's a man here who's attached to a machine.
It's awful. But he's so annoying. He's constantly
saying to the girls, 'Lady, lady, I want to sleep.
Lady, lady, I want to eat.' He just wants attention.
And the girls are so nice to him. But you can't
satisfy him. He's always yelling. It's so sad.
One day I couldn't stand it. I said to him,
'You know what you are? You're a CPA!'[2]
But he didn't know what I was talking about!"

---

[2]constant pain in the ass

November 2004

VISIT 21

"You'll laugh when you hear what I just did,"
my mother said gleefully.
"What?" I asked, knowing she had just participated
in the memories project.
"I just had a paintbrush in my hand! I painted!"
I laughed at her fervor.
"You see—I told you you'd laugh!" she said,
pointing her index finger at me.
"I'm laughing at your reaction. I think it's great!
What did you paint?"
"I wasn't going to try anything hard
like a squash or a pumpkin. I painted an apple.
I was glad when the paintbrush
produced an apple!"
"You don't have to worry. Just have fun."
"What do you mean? You have to have
some ability! I don't know how they convinced me
to do this. I told them to wait for Dee."
"They want you, not me. It's just about
having fun with the paint."
"Well, I don't know what I'll do next week.
But I'm not going to worry. That's next week."

VISIT 22

"Did you have your art class today?"
I asked my mother.
"Yes. I made a mess! I told her not to take me!
What a mess I made!"
"What did you paint?"
"I was supposed to draw a jar of string beans.
I couldn't get the string beans stringy.
They were fat. I'm sure they won't ask me again."
"I'm sure you'll get asked back."
"I won't accept. Enough is enough.
One artist in the family is enough!"

VISIT 23

My mother was in bed trying to pull the sheet
over her eyes when I arrived.
"That light is bothering me. I was trying to nap,"
she said, pointing to the ceiling light
on her roommate's side of the room,
shining through the mesh top
of the room divider curtain. "She doesn't need
that light to read. She can use her wall light.
I read with just my wall light. That's enough.
But the nurse said she had to have the ceiling light
to read. She called me a dirty Jew!"
"Who did?"
"The nurse."
"Why?"
"I don't know. She said my partner needs
the ceiling light. She reads her Bible."
"Well, I can turn it off now because she is sleeping."

Nurse Report: "Your mother slid out of her wheelchair last
night but she was OK. She was joking about it."

VISIT 24

"I didn't sleep very well," my mother said.
"There was a group of workers singing out there.
They kept singing and singing and I couldn't sleep.
Finally I sang with them. 'Over there, over there.'
Then they got into a fight. So much noise.
I couldn't sleep. It's funny. I hear them
when I'm in the country and I used to hear
that family singing next door when I was
in the suburbs."

December 2004

VISIT 25

"You know that woman who wears
the funny clothes? I told them she should be
in charge of changing the daily calendar
and weather. The girls get behind.
She's up early and out here and she'd be efficient.
So now she's doing it and it's much better.
You know, I think she wears all those tops
because she doesn't trust anyone. So she puts on
everything she owns."

VISIT 26

"I told them to stop parking people in wheelchairs
in the hall. You can't get by. You need
a free and clear hallway. Did you notice no one
was sitting there anymore? Freedom and liberty,"
she said, waving her arms in the air.
"Free and clear! They're going to throw me
out of here!"

VISIT 27

"You see him?" my mother said,
pointing to a hunched-over man
staring blankly ahead, walking
into the room. "He's much better.
They have someone different with him
every day. They take him for walks
all the time."
"How has he improved?"
"He's happier, not so grumpy.
But it's not fair. Everyone
would like that kind of attention."

VISIT 28

"Here is some pudding for you, Eleanor,"
the head nurse said to a resident
in a wheelchair near my mother.
"Good for you!" she acknowledged
when Eleanor swallowed the pudding,
pills and all. She bent over and kissed her.
"You see what they do here?" my mother said.
"They kiss them and stroke them.
If they didn't eat, that's it! I wouldn't give in
to them. They'd learn to take it themselves."
"I think they're doing the best they can," I say.
"You don't think they'd learn to take it themselves?"
"No."

Nurse Report: "I went in to give you Mom her meds. She
said, 'You're always giving me pills, pills. That's all you ever
give me. Why don't you give me a kiss?' I can give you both,
I told her. And I did. I gave her a big kiss on her cheek.
She smiled."

January 2005

VISIT 29

"I want you to take Tim home with you,"
my mother told Charlie. "He'll help you garden.
Just bring him back by 4:30. Here,
you can wheel him out this door.
They won't miss him. He'll help you.
He knows gardening. Just bring him back
by 4:30 for dinner."
"I can't take him with me," Charlie said.
"Yes you can. Look. Just take him out
the back door. He knows gardening.
He's Italian."

VISIT 30

"Last night Tim wouldn't eat. So,
I fed him a piece of my melon
and he ate it. I talk to him. I try
to draw him out. He talks to me.
I can't understand what he's saying,
but I talk to him. I try to give him hope."

VISIT 31

"You'll never believe what your mother did,"
my mother said, covering her face
with her hands. "I can't believe it!"
"What did you do?"
"I must have had a dream. I got up
during the night and put on my robe
and went down to the nurses' station
because I thought a woman had fallen
and I had to make a report. The nurse said,
no, that hadn't happened
and I didn't have to make a report
and I should go back to bed.
And she was right. I must have visualized it
as though it really happened.
It was so real to me. That's not normal."

VISIT 32

"Grandma, why is your ring on the table?"
Holly asked.
"Because I want to leave it for Emily."
"But it can be stolen, Grandma.
You should never take it off!"
"I know, but it came to me this morning
that they were coming for me today.
So I took it off to leave for Emily.
It's the only other thing I have to give her.
I gave you my high school medal."
"I know Grandma, but you have to keep your ring
on your finger all the time."
"I don't know what got into me today.
All day I was waiting for them to come for me."
"To go where?"
"To my final resting place.
Finally, I asked one of the girls about it.
She didn't know anything. I said,
'Whom can I ask?' She referred me
to another girl. She didn't know either
and said I should talk to the head nurse,
so I did. She said no one was coming for me today.
So here I am. I think I have bats in my belfry."

Nurse Report: "I always talk with your Mom about books.
We talked about Nelson Mandela the other day. She's reading
about him. She's pretty savvy. I always make her laugh."

VISIT 33

"I'm not happy here."
"What's the matter?"
"My partner keeps the light on
'til twelve o'clock and I can't get to sleep.
It shines in my eyes. So they told her
she has to turn it off by eleven,
but that's too late too. She reads.
One of the girls told me that when I agreed
to come here I had to accept everything
that goes on here."
"That's not true. You certainly do have rights.
The staff wants to know if you're unhappy.
They try to make things better."
"But I don't want to be the bad guy.
I feel peculiar."
"You're as entitled as anyone to be comfortable
here. So go ahead and be the bad guy!"
She laughed.

February 2005

VISIT 34

"I heard you drew in pencil
in your art class last week."
"Oh, that," my mother said, waving her hand.
"I don't remember."
"Did you draw a butterfly?"
"Yes."
"What else?"
"Oh, a basket—a basket, not a bastard,"
she said, smiling, putting her index finger
to her lips, whispering "shh,"
looking around impishly
to see if anyone had heard.
"But I don't like painting. I make a mess."

Director Report: "I wheeled your mother past Tim's room.
She said, 'Tim is gone, isn't he?' 'Yes,' I replied. 'I will miss
him,' she said."

VISIT 35

"The clock is gone.
The one that was over there,"
my mother said, pointing to the top
of her roommate's TV.
"I could see it from bed.
They said they'd replace it,
but it's been five days.
They could put it up there,"
she said, pointing to the top of the closet.
"They won't replace it, Mom.
It belonged to Helen. They had to unplug it
because the radio part kept playing."
"No, it wasn't hers. It's supplied by the place."
"Mom, they don't supply clocks here. I checked."
"Well, that's a new one. You can't trust anyone."

VISIT 36

"My partner left."
"I know. They changed her room
so you can get a more compatible roommate
who will turn the light out at nine
like you like to do."
"Well, I won't let the girls who sided with her
help me."
"You mean the ones who said she could keep
her light on at night?"
"Yes. I tell them, 'I don't want you.
Send someone else.' And they do
send someone else and those girls
are very nice to me."

Nurse Report: "I went in to give your Mom her meds. She
was grumpy. She said, 'I don't want to be bothered. If you
were in my place you'd feel the same way.' And I couldn't
argue with her."

VISIT 37

When I woke my mother, she pulled the covers
over her head.
"What's going on, Mom?"
"I have nothing. That's what's going on."
"What do you mean?"
"I have nothing. They have everything.
We get a nibble. They have it all.
I have to get out of here."
"Who is 'they'?"
"You know. Them. Look."
"Look at what?"
"That."
"This alarm button?"
"Yes. They keep tabs on everything you do.
You have to know what's going on
when you pick a place like this. Otherwise,
you find out when it's too late.
I don't know what I'm going to do."
"Mom, here's a photo album for you
with pictures from your birthday party
and Joseph and Carol's visit."
"Well, that was from before.
It's not like that anymore.
We get nothing. You get it?"
"Yes, I get it. But, you know, Mom,
you have to be strong. You have to do your part.
Come on, now. Get up. I'll comb your hair."
"When am I going to get my hair cut?"
"I'll check on that while you get washed up."
"You'll have to stay all day so we can see
what we're going to do."

VISIT 38

"I haven't been able to find my slippers.
I looked everywhere. The laundry
checked and couldn't find them.
The other day I saw another woman
wearing them. I told one of the girls
those were my slippers. She said,
'I'll see about it.' Then she told me
the other woman got two pairs of slippers
for Christmas and they were hers.
But then the laundry found them."
"So you have them back?"
"Yes. But now my sweater's missing.
I asked my old partner if she had it.
She said, 'Yes, what do you want me
to do with it?' I thought she could hang it
on my doorknob when she went by.
But she never did, so I asked her again.
While I was talking to her, someone
pulled my wheelchair back and said,
'We'll take care of it for you. Don't bother her.'
Can you imagine! We can't even talk
for ourselves! And they are so kissy-huggy here.
So permissive! They let people do whatever
they want! You see her over there,
sleeping with her mouth open?
She used to stay in her room all the time.
Now she walks around and puts things
under her blouse. I said to her, 'What
are you looking for? Go back to your room!'
I'm so annoyed. There's no discipline here!"

Nurse Report: "Your mother slapped a woman in the hall. I
don't know what precipitated it. I don't think she likes that
woman."

March 2005

VISIT 39

"This is the weirdest place I've ever been in."
"What do you mean?"
"They're very lackadaisical here."
"Who?"
"The girls. They just go along, 'round and 'round,
yes, yes, no, no. It doesn't matter."
"The nurses?"
"No. Well, they give you pills.
But they don't tell you anything unless you ask.
I ask what are these pills for? They don't know."
"They're for your blood pressure and memory
and nerves, Mom."
"I told them I got injections for blood pressure
and I'm satisfied with that."
"You never got injections. You always
had pills. Remember Dr. James gave you samples
of Norvasc?"
"No, I got injections. I told them I don't want
the pills. They may be causing my rash.
They're just not authentic here."
"They're kind."
"Yes, they're very kind, very nice, very good
to us. But if someone asks for chewing gum,
they get it—or an ice pop. Whatever snack
they want, they get."
"What's wrong with that?"
"It's all sugar. There's no control here.
Nobody gets better. Nobody gets discharged."
"They're ill, Mom. They need care.
Where should they go?"
"They're not ill. They're fine.
They just stay. They just go on and on."

VISIT 40

"I'm so cranky and crabby in the morning.
But this girl knows just what to do,
just what I want. I can't get over it!
I ask her, 'How do you know what to do?'
She says her mother taught her.
I'm grumpy and it doesn't faze her.
She just goes about her business
and knows what I want. She's terrific.
Can you imagine?"

VISIT 41

"There are new people here.
They don't know what to do.
They don't know what to see.
They don't know what they're doing.
They don't belong here.
They should go home with their medicine."
"They're ill, Mom. They need help.
Who would take care of them?"
"I don't know.
They should be somewhere else."

Nurse Report: "Your mother and I have a good time together in the morning. I get her set, comb her hair; we talk."

"My mother loves you. She's amazed you know just what she wants."

"I told her my mother taught me. She was an LNA for ten years and loved taking care of people."

"Bless you both."

VISIT 42

At the dermatologist:
"I read in this magazine that certain things
are good for certain things. It said
that chocolate is good for the skin.
So I've been eating chocolate,"
my mother said, grinning.
"How much do you have?"
"I only allow myself two small squares.
Two in the morning and two at night."
"Does it help your rash?"
"For a little while. Do you see that one
over there?"
"The receptionist?"
"Yes. If she wasn't blonde
she wouldn't have a job."

VISIT 43

"How are you enjoying your Ethan Allen book?"
"I'm not."
"It's history?"
"No, it's about him and how things came about here."

April 2005

VISIT 44

"You see that woman to your right?
She used to be a horror! But she's changed.
She's calmed down. Now she's quiet
and civil. So I tried to be a little friendly
toward her. But she doesn't respond."

VISIT 45

I add more Depends, Prevail underpads
to my mother's supply,
bang the closet door shut,
unbrake her wheelchair, screech it
from her bedside, draw up the armchair,
legs scraping the floor—in the hope
my mother would wake up.
I nudge her finally—call "Mom"
and she wakes.
"I've been sleeping so long,"
her eyes blinking, closing,
opening, closing,
sleeping once more.
I sit, knit two rows of an afghan,
nudge her again.
"I've been sleeping since lunch,"
her eyes opening, closing, sleeping again.
I knit three more rows, stare
at the family photos crowning her head.
"Mom," yet again.
She rolls over on her back.
"I've been sleeping and sleeping.
It doesn't ask you what you want.
It just comes," she says.
And she slept.

Nurse Report: "Your mother slapped another resident and
pulled her hair. We had to take her to her room. She said she
was better off there."

VISIT 46

"Do birds grow from trees?"
"No, they don't."
"Well, I keep seeing a bird
growing out of a branch out there.
She has no wings to fly yet.
Look. Look up there. You see that bird?"
"No, I don't."
"There, up there."
"That's a knot on the branch."
"It's not a bird?"
"No, it's a knot that's sticking up."
"Well, can you see why I thought it was a bird?"

VISIT 47

"How are you doing, Mom?"
"Okay. I like the sunshine.
It feels good. I don't go down
to breakfast. I like to sit here in the sun."
"Yes, the sun feels good in the winter."
"I never would have imagined
when I was in school that I'd wind up
in Vermont."
"I know. Me, either. You never know
what's around the corner."
"When I was young, we did.
I always thought New York was so big.
It had everything to offer."

Director Report: "Your mother had a rough weekend—was verbally abusive to residents—made fun of them—of staff and visitors, too—tried to kick a resident, pulled her hair, was wheeled to her room, fighting and screaming— has been refusing her meds. How do you feel about crushing her meds in her tea?"

"Absolutely. No qualms about that."
"We have a call in to her doctor."

VISIT 48

"You see that?" my mother said,
pointing to the ceiling sprinkler.
"They're listening to us."
"No, Mom. It's a sprinkler in case of fire."
"They're everywhere."
"Of course. In case of fire."
"No, they're for both."

VISIT 49

"There were no parking spaces out front
this morning," I said to my mother.
"Well, maybe it's because we had a cut-off
last night—those who are older
were leaving and the newer ones staying.
A lady came up to me and said
I was one of the ones staying.
And I didn't care, but a lot of people
were upset. It's hard for someone like me.
I'm not tolerant. It isn't good.
But I could give some of them
a kick in the pants. It's good
I'm not on the committee that decides
who leaves and stays. The girls
all tootsie up to these people
when I think they'd like to give them
a kick in the pants."
"I think they try to be understanding."
"Well, I'm too intolerant.
I'm trying to be better, but I just wish
some of them would go."

May 2005

VISIT 50

"And they keep on trying to give me pills."
"Well, your blood pressure medicine is important.
You don't want to have a stroke."
"I don't believe that. This is the only place
I've ever been in that pushes pills like that."

VISIT 51

"How are things going, Mom?"
"So-so."
"What's happening?"
"My roommate has three big stuffed dogs
on top of the chifforobe.
The kids don't like it."
"What kids?"
"My kids. They make a to-do about it.
Of course, I have to wait until Al comes home.
He's part of it, too. But it is all going to blow up."

Nurse Report: "I'd like to order liquid morphine for your mother because of her blisters. She screams when anyone tries to touch her."

"What about something less extreme, like Percocet?"

"The morphine is liquid and we have a better chance of getting it down her."

"Can you give it to her only at 'personal care' time?"

"Yes."

VISIT 52

"I hear you're not taking your meds."
"I'm not a medicine gal. I think
the itches have gone away
since I stopped taking all that crap.
They peddle these pills; I think
it makes them feel good.
I don't know what it does for us."

VISIT 53

"It's a funny thing. We had a meeting
and decided the older residents should leave.
They've been here too long. They do
whatever they want. So we said good-bye
to them, but then they didn't leave.
They don't dress right.
They have to be fed.
They do whatever they want.
The committee met and we decided
they should go home with their medications
and the next day they're still here.
I should have stayed in the other wing."

Nurse Report: "Your mother hasn't gotten out of bed
for two days. She's refusing food and drink and says she
wants to die. She's refused her meds. Her doctor has pre-
scribed liquid Prozac so she can take it in a drink or food. If
this continues, it may be the beginning of the end. You may
want to contact hospice. We'll see how it goes."

VISIT 54

"I'm supposed to marry this new guy.
It's going to be a big shindig. The whole place
is invited. But there's a big to-do
because I don't want to invite THAT woman—
I hate her and I don't want her there
and the girls are all very nice to her
and they say she has to come.
I won't come if she's there."
"Well, if you're the bride how can you
be absent?"
"Well, there's going to be a blow-out
because I don't want her to come."

June 2005

VISIT 55

I wheeled my mother out to the courtyard.
We sat under an awning.
"I watch the others," she said.
"They do nothing. It drives me nuts.
It's amazing. They sleep. They're in bed.
They read. And I go along with it.
They open to any page and read something.
It doesn't matter what. It's not historical.
And I mumble along. On Sunday,
at the service, they just read. It's boring.
I marvel at what they do. They're doing nothing.
They just open a book and read something.
Anything. And I read and it doesn't mean anything.
Why are they taking those girls for a walk?"
"It's a beautiful day."
"So what? Who cares. It doesn't matter.
Nothing matters."

VISIT 56

"My books are my friends.
I always like to have them around me.
But I can't read that one about Etty Hilesun.
It's too disturbing."

VISIT 57

"Did you know the Caressa group?"
"No."
"She's something, Caressa.
She's so delicate," she said,
making an "o" with her thumb
and index finger.
"I get a sparkle in my eye
when I think of her."

VISIT 58

"Hi, Mom!"
Mom opened her eyes.
"Get out! I don't want to talk to anyone."
I put away the Prevail underpads,
the disposable washcloths, Olay body wash
for extra dry skin, all labeled with her name,
hung up clothes that had dropped to the bottom
of her closet.
"Mom?"
"What do you want?"
"Would you like a short visit?"
"No! Get out!"

Nurse Report: "On the way to the dermatologist your mother asked me if we were going to Europe. I told her we were going to the dermatologist and we were almost there. She said, 'Why do I have to go to the doctor? They don't do anything for me.' But when we came home she said they did do something for her."

VISIT 59

"Hi, Mom," Charlie said.
She opened her eyes.
"Get out! I don't want to talk."
"Would you like a little visit?"
"No!"

July 2005

VISIT 60

"How are you, Mom?"
"How should I be?"
She winces.
"Is it your blisters?"
"That's the least of the problems."
"What is the problem?"
"I can't tell you. Some things
are too personal to talk about."
"You're shivering. Are you cold?"
She nods her head yes.
"Here's another blanket."
"Those dogs up there bother me."
"They're stuffed animals, Mom."
"I know. But it's something
about those images…I can't explain.
They do something to me."

Nurse Report: "Your mother had a hard night last night. She was sitting at the edge of her bed at 11:30, quite agitated. They couldn't get her to lie down. So they brought her to the sitting room, and she stayed there almost all night. We called the on-call doctor, and he ordered an anti-psychotic. She calmed down and went back to bed finally. I think the Prednisone is playing with her head, too.

Later: "Your mother was doing well this morning, socializing in the sitting room. But she got increasingly agitated as the day went on, so we had to take her back to her room, screaming and kicking and hitting."

VISIT 61

"Hi, Mom."
Eyes open. "Get out!
I don't want to talk to you!"
Eyes close.

VISIT 62

"I can't believe I've lived this long."
"You're the last of the Mohicans."
"Yes. We had dinner—about three or four
of us, right here."
"Uh-huh."
"But I can't believe I'm living this long."
"How was your lunch?"
"Pretty good. We have a little from here,
a little from there. It's like that.
We had our dinner here at this table.
About four of us."
"Have you been reading, Mom?"
"Not much. I never expected to live this long.
My stepmother used to say that, too."

VISIT 63

"Hi, Mom."
Eyes open. "Get out!
I don't want to talk!"
Eyes close.
"Can we visit for a few minutes?"
Eyes open. "No, get out!"
Eyes close.

Nurse Report: "Your mother was agitated yesterday. She pinched another woman. The other woman hit her. No one was hurt. We took your mother to her room but she came out again. We watched her carefully. She needs more hearing aid batteries."

VISIT 64

"Mom, we're planning Holly's wedding."
"Isn't Holly married to you?"
"No, I'm married to Charlie.
We're planning a wedding at our house.
Will you come?"
"I guess so.
Isn't she married already?"
"No."

VISIT 65

"Hi, Mom. What's new?"
"I'm not going with the new.
I have enough of the old to deal with."
"You had a nice lunch."
"Yes. You get filled up quickly here.
This morning we had a weighing thing.
I don't know what you call it."
"You mean you got weighed?"
"No. Our food intake got weighed."

Nurse Report: "Your mother was agitated this evening during dinner. She was repeatedly yelling at two others at her table: 'Stop drinking and eat your dinner!' One of them was actually on a puree diet, but your mother couldn't understand that. We took her to her room before she could assault them and she's finishing her dinner there now. It's the same two that upset her so we're going to change her seating. She complained of pain and I was able to get her to take something for it but she couldn't explain to me what was bothering her. I called her doctor to give her a low dosage of Haloperidol to calm her down because I'm afraid she may act out when the staff gets her ready for bed."

August 2005

VISIT 66

"Your blisters are gone, Mom.
The medicine is working."
"They're almost gone."
"Most of them are."
"Every morning they want me
to take the medicine."
"Well, look, it's working."
"I don't know. It's a trial for me."
"What do you mean?"
"There are so many doctors on this case.
And I'm alone."
"Why?"
"I don't know. Everyone is against me.
It's because of the medication."
"Who cares what you're taking?"
"I don't know. I'm alone."
"How do you know?"
"This tells me. In here," she says,
poking her right index finger at her heart.
"I don't know how I got here.
I never should have come.
I don't want to be here.
I don't want to be.
Maybe I'll perish.
That will be all right with me.
I don't want acclamation, decoration, fabrication!
I'm not a blackberry, a raspberry, an elderberry!"

VISIT 67

"Mom, next week is your birthday.
You'll be 93. Emily will be here.
We'll have a birthday party."
"Oh, Dee, I don't want a party.
No more birthdays. I don't want
any more birthdays. It's enough already.
Besides, I'm often in bed all day."

Nurse Report: "Your mother was agitated again today. She
threw her cranberry juice at a resident. She demanded the
staff stand with faces against the wall. She said if she got
hold of them she'd wring their necks. We ordered one-half
milligram of Haloperidol to calm her down."

VISIT 68

"The girls here are very nice.
I don't say anything about it
if they forget to do something
because they're so nice.
I never complain.
They never hear it from me."

VISIT 69

"I don't go downstairs very much anymore.
Sometimes I feel like it; sometimes I don't.
There's a woman who sits in the same chair
out there all the time. I don't like her.
But the girls love her. They always take her side.
She just sits there. Her eyes go this way
and that. I wish she wasn't there. But there
she is. They always fuss over her
and give her attention. They just leave me
alone. No one comes to check on me here.
Just once in a while a girl comes in
and says hello and asks how I'm doing."

THE LAST VISIT

"I don't read anymore. I don't know why.
I have so many nice books. I wish I did.
But I just don't get around to it."

Director Report: "I got a call from the charge nurse tonight.
Your mother got agitated in the day room at dinner and
jabbed another resident with a fork and drew blood. The
doctor on call ordered an injection of Haloperidol to calm
her down and we took her to her room. We have a call in to
her doctor to put her back on Aracept. She's been calmer
recently although she often evinces the biting commentary.
When the day room is crowded she doesn't seem to handle it
too well. It's best to keep her out of the crowd. She can eat
on a tray table in the hall rather than at the round table. I'll
call the family of the woman she stabbed. She's all right. She's
up-to-date on her tetanus. Don't feel badly about it. It's part
of your mother's disease. The other family will understand
this, too, and we will take care of it."

Nurse Report: "We have some bad news for you. Your mother
died this afternoon. She complained of heartburn. We sat her
up, made her comfortable. She refused any medication. When
we returned to check on her, she was gone. We are all so
shocked and so sorry."

Ruth Tornberg Klein
died on the afternoon of August 11, 2005,
the day before we were to celebrate her ninety-third birthday.
A brain autopsy revealed she had Alzheimer's Disease.

Epilogue

Staff Memories

Sharon: "Your mother was a wise, thoughtful woman and very much in the moment. Her disease put a negative spin on her perceptions and caused an inability to express her thoughts at times. She'd hallucinate but then she'd come back into lucidity. She'd suffer, but then come back into the moment. She'd suffer and then go back to her reading. Dementia isn't usually a back-and-forth situation in my experience. Once someone starts sliding mentally, they keep on going downhill."

Fran: "I miss the old man. Where is he?" Fran asked as we were cleaning out my mother's room. "I have him," I said. "He hung in my parents' living room for many years." "Your mom would say, 'He keeps me safe. He protects me.' I'll miss talking to her about books."

Kate: "I'll miss your mother. She made my life interesting."

Sherry: "Ruth was such a breath of fresh air. She was very near and dear to my heart and I will never forget her. She was a treasure."

Dale: "I will miss Ruth. She was a good woman."

Kerrie: "Thanks so much for Ruth. She was a wonderful lady."

Chaplain Laura: "I saw your Mom the day before she died. I asked her how she was doing. She said, 'So-so—but then I don't do anything about it, so what can you expect?'

"When she first came to the nursing home, she noticed me talking to others. I usually don't talk to residents right away. I give them a chance to settle in. When I finally did go over to her, she said, 'I thought you wouldn't talk to me.' That was because of my collar and cross.

"Once when they were playing bingo in the rec room, I asked her if she wanted to go in. She said, 'no.' 'You don't care for Bingo?' I asked. 'You mean idiot's delight?' she said.

"I used to take her for walks on the trail. We'd pick a pine cone or a Queen Anne's lace or an herb for her to smell and she'd put them in her lap and take them back to her room.

"I always hugged her and held her hand while we talked. This last time I saw her, she took my hand to her lap and held it there. She had trouble with my cross and collar, but she overcame it. She said, 'We're friends. I love you.'"

The Difference

She was there
as she always was.
The nurse said
she was in bed
as though sleeping.
The white curtain
was drawn around her.
The woven blanket
covered her, each arm
lying above it.
She looked as though
she was sleeping, except—
her face was gray,
her eyes sealed shut,
her lips lightly parted.

Things weren't so different
from all the other times.
Everything was in its place—
the bulletin board of photos
of children, grandchildren,
great-grandchild,
the painting of "The Old Man,"
the one she said "protected" her,
the Hadassah magazine,
the biography of Etty Hilesun
on the nightstand,
the TV she never watched,
the bird feeder outside her window.

I stroked her hair, laid my cheek
against her forehead,
silently mentioned my sorrow
at her unrealized life,
the difficulties in our relationship.
I took her hand. It was soft and cold.
Then I saw the ring—
the bulky, Yemenite ring
with the large turquoise stone
she found one day in a jumble
of jewelry in a cosmetic bag,
given her by a cousin,
that attracted much attention—
and gently I removed it
from her finger.
I wanted her to wake up
and talk to me as always.
Surely she would open her eyes.
Surely she would know
I didn't want to let her go.
Surely she would tell me another story.
She was my mother.

Mother's Day 2006

At the drugstore,
Mother's Day cards
are on display.
I have the familiar impulse
to buy one.
Then I remember
I will not be needing
a Mother's Day card
this year.
Something tumbles down
in my chest.

The newspapers offer
Mother's Day brunch, dinner,
diamonds, jewelry,
lingerie, books.
I stare at them,
recalling the year
I bought her coral-colored
toilet water in a fat oval bottle
with a tall neck
for thirty-five cents at Woolworth's
and my step-grandmother
said what a waste of money;
the years of Girl Scout-made
bookmarks, change purses, cards;
the years of nightgowns, scarves,
sweaters, and books,
hoping for the favorable response,
not the minimal or negative reception—

not the I-don't-need-any-more-books-
I-have-too-many-already.
Toward the end,
with few things needed,
we gave her a flower-bouquet-a-month.
These she loved.

I see the ads for Mother's Day
in the shop windows
and reminisce how I knew
her colors, her styles,
could shop for her at the end,
knew her loves,
knew what things I could say
to share our similar humor.

I hadn't thought ahead
to the first Mother's Day without her—
how it would rub the loss.